スタジオジブリ
STUDIO GHIBLI

Studio Ghibli is a Tokyo-based animation film studio founded in 1985 by directors Isao Takahata and Hayao Miyazaki. The studio has produced more than twenty feature-length films, many of which have garnered numerous awards and critical acclaim, including *My Neighbor Totoro*, *Kiki's Delivery Service*, *Princess Mononoke*, and the Academy Award–winning *Spirited Away*. The studio earned four consecutive Academy Award nominations for Best Animated Feature Film for *The Wind Rises*, *The Tale of The Princess Kaguya*, *When Marnie Was There*, and *The Red Turtle*. *Earwig and the Witch* was an official selection for the 2020 Cannes Film Festival. *The Boy and the Heron* was released in 2023.

Licensed by Studio Ghibli.
STUDIO GHIBLI™ is a trademark of Studio Ghibli Inc.
Manufactured for Chronicle Books LLC in 2024.
Copyright © 1989 Eiko Kadono - Studio Ghibli - N
All rights reserved.

ISBN 978-1-7972-3014-6

FSC
www.fsc.org

MIX
Paper from
responsible sources
FSC™ C169962

Manufactured in China.

10 9 8 7 6 5 4 3 2 1

CHRONICLE BOOKS
680 SECOND STREET
SAN FRANCISCO CA 94107
CHRONICLEBOOKS.COM